RAILWAY KNITTING
WORKBOOK

The Journey Continues

BY DELA WILKINS

FriesenPress

Suite 300 - 990 Fort St
Victoria, BC, Canada, V8V 3K2
www.friesenpress.com

Copyright © 2015 by Dela Wilkins
First Edition — 2015

ISBN
978-1-4602-5789-0 (Hardcover)
978-1-4602-5790-6 (Paperback)
978-1-4602-5791-3 (eBook)

1. Crafts & Hobbies, Needlework, Crocheting

Distributed to the trade by The Ingram Book Company

Library and Archives Canada Cataloguing in Publication Wilkins, Dela, 1949-, author

Railway knitting workbook : the journey continues / Dela Wilkins,
author ; Freyja Zazu, illustrator. -- First edition.

Issued in print and electronic formats.
ISBN 978-1-4602-5789-0 (bound).--ISBN 978-1-4602-5790-6 (pbk.).—
ISBN 978-1-4602-5791-3 (ebook)

1. Crocheting. 2. Knitting. I. Zazu, Freyja, illustrator II. Title.

TT820.W55 2015   746.43   C2015-900554-X

C2015-900555-8

Table of Contents

Illustrations by Freyja Zazu, Victoria, BC Canada

Photos by Dela Wilkins except page 2 and 38 by RK Wilkins

This book is dedicated to the memory of my mother, Henny Van Essen. Her hands taught mine.

Acknowledgements

Thank you to my Railway Knitting colleagues: Catherine Mick and Mary Tanti.

Thank you to my quality control team: Robin Cook, Spencer Diamond, and Karen Lancey.

A special thank you to my father Peter Van Essen. He knows why.

RAILWAY KNITTING

The origin of the term *Railway Knitting* as another name for Tunisian crochet dates back to the 1880s. The name likely comes from the appearance of the Tunisian Simple Stitch which looks like railway lines and railway ties. I find it an appropriate technique to work with on the train when I travel between Vancouver, British Columbia and Toronto, Ontario; an 84-hour journey across five Canadian provinces.

A few years ago I found myself offering impromptu activity sessions on the train trips. This hands-on activity was formalized in 2011 as part of the *Artists On Board Program* with VIA Rail. The technique appeals to both knitters and crocheters and is not difficult for a first-timer to learn.

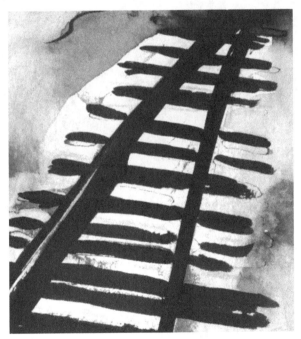

Tunisian crochet resembles railway lines and ties.

My approach to teaching Railway Knitting techniques is to help the learner to understand the structure and direction of the stitches and to think about opportunities for hook placement and yarn choices. On the train we have only a few hours each day to meet in the activity car. I will rarely see any of the participants again after the end of the trip, as they come from many different countries and speak several different languages. It is interesting to see how a hands-on activity overcomes language and cultural barriers. During our trip together, we are a community of knitters and crocheters.

As a child I learned needlework techniques from my mother, including the Tunisian crochet technique she called *Tunische haaksteek*. Needlework was a school subject for her, growing up in the Netherlands in the 1930s. The Tunisian knit stitch was called a *tricotsteek* and looks like stockinette in knitting.

Most of my relatives who did needlework transitioned effortlessly between sewing, embroidery, knitting, crochet, and Tunisian crochet. They often worked without patterns. Children would stand still long enough to be measured; they would have a hand or foot traced onto a scrap of paper with their name and the date, and sooner or later a sweater or a pair of mittens or socks would appear. I remember watching my Oma in 1959 as she was knitting a pleated skirt for me, her oldest granddaughter in Canada. I leaned over her shoulder for hours to watch her hands at work.

My first design in Tunisian crochet was the bodice of a full-length crocheted formal dress with puff sleeves, in 1972.

Tunisian Simple Stitch bodice of a formal crocheted dress. 1972.

The Tunisian Simple Stitch provided a closer fabric for the bodice than the open crochet work of the skirt and sleeves. I wore this at my parents' anniversary that year.

Tunisian crochet in a formal dress. The author with her mother. 1972.

The most interesting garment I have worked on is a vest which my mother and I worked on together. We used a favorite well-fitting garment as the pattern base. We discovered that we both crocheted to the same gauge, so we were able to complete the garment quickly. Apparently my mother and her mother, my Oma, could also work on garments together.

Use a garment as the pattern for a vest.

Tunisian Crochet

In 2010 I discovered the *Encyclopedia of Tunisian Crochet (*LoneStar Abilene Publishing, LLC, 2004*)* by *Angela "Arnie" Grabowski.* I was surprised to learn that there are more than 400 ways to make stitches in Tunisian crochet. I set out to learn them all. Many of the stitches from the book are available on her website, ChezCrochet.com.

Some of my attempts to work new stitches were what some might call a "failure", but I saw these as an opportunity to explore more variations.

My favorite questions became: What happens if I do this…? What happens if I change colours here? What if I work this stitch in the round?

For two years I explored print and online resources in Tunisian crochet to find the origins of the technique and made notes of my own questions, explorations, and discoveries. Seeing a rule, such as *"Never turn your work,"* would make me ask what happens if I *do* turn the work?

This workbook is the result of my personal experience looking into the many possibilities working with Tunisian crochet stitches. Some of the techniques presented here can be worked with a regular crochet hook. Other techniques require an afghan hook or a double-ended hook. Many of the techniques are a result of my knowledge in other needlework techniques. I explored whether some of those techniques could be successfully applied to Tunisian crochet.

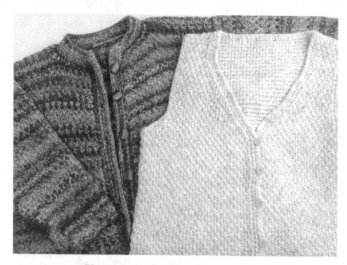

Honeycomb stitch garments.

The Basic Stitches (review from *Railway Knitting 2012*)

Tunisian Crochet is the term to use when searching for library or Internet resources. Stitch names are not consistent in Tunisian crochet, so it is always best to read the description of the stitch in a pattern and practice it in a test sample. There are different names for the same stitch in American and British crochet patterns. Some stitch dictionaries number a stitch rather than name it. In this review my previous descriptions of the Purl and the Reverse stitches have been updated to the 2014 stitch names.

Edge Stitches: The first stitch and the last stitch are considered edge stitches and form a selvedge or self-edge. The selvedge stitches have a different appearance from the other stitches in the same row. They are not usually part of the pattern stitches.

Tunisian Simple Stitch (TSS): Slide the hook behind the front vertical stitch, keeping the hook at the front of the work. Wrap the Yarn over the Hook (YOH), and pull up a loop. Keep the loop on the hook.

Tunisian Purl Stitch (TPS): Bring the working yarn to the front of the row, between the stitch on the hook and the next stitch to be picked up. Slide the hook behind the front vertical stitch as in the TSS. Bring the working yarn under the hook to the back. Wrap the YOH, and pull up a loop. The Forward Pass yarn forms a knob in front of the stitch.

Tunisian Moss Stitch or Honeycomb pattern: Work one TSS, then one TPS, alternating across the row. On the next row position the stitches above their opposites. The fabric does not roll up because the yarn alternates from the back to the front of the row for each stitch.

Honeycomb stitch pattern.

This stitch combination is effective when you use two colours, changing them at the beginning of the Return Pass. If you place the stitches above each other in columns you will get a different pattern.

Tunisian Reverse Stitch (TRS): Tilt the work toward you, peek over the top edge to locate the back vertical portion of the stitch. Slide the hook behind the back vertical stitch. Keep the hook along the back of the fabric. Wrap the YOH and pull up a loop.

Tunisian Knit Stitch (TKS): Insert the hook from the front through to the back of the work into the space between the front vertical and back vertical parts of the same stitch. Wrap the YOH, pull up a loop. A thick ridge forms on the back because the yarn is wrapped around the previous Return Pass.

Tunisian Full Stitch or Waffle Stitch (TFS): Insert the hook from the front to the back of the work into the space between two stitches. Because this stitch is worked into the spaces between stitches, it should be worked either *before* each stitch or *after* each stitch.

This means in one row you will start working between stitch one and two (*before* the second stitch) and the space between the last two stitches at the far end is *not* worked. In the next row, the space between one and two is *not* worked (working *after* the second stitch), but the last space is worked. This will balance the row.

Both the TKS and TFS have some stretch in a south/north direction.

Tunisian Twisted Simple Stitch: Enter the stitch from the opposite direction by hooking it, and then twist the hook to pick up the loop. It makes a difference if you twist the hook up or down, so be consistent in your directions.

Tunisian Extended Stitches: Any of these basic stitches can be extended by adding one chain stitch above the loop on the hook.

Extended simple stitch in three colours on an afghan hook. Change colours at each end.

Extended simple stitch with a double-ended hook. One colour for all Forward Pass stitches; a second colour for the Return Pass stitches.

The Foundation Row

Tunisian crochet stitches are started into a base row or first row called a **Foundation Row.** The foundation row is most often a row of Tunisian Simple Stitches on the Forward Pass and a chain row for the Return Pass. The pattern will begin in Row 2 and will change the appearance of Row 1.

When you learn to recognize the stitch construction and the direction of the working rows, you can move on to explore other stitch options.

Components of the Tunisian Simple Stitch in a Foundation Row:

- The **front vertical** and the **back vertical** are made by the loop on the Forward Pass.
- On the Return Pass the **back bump** on the horizontal chain catches the loop and holds it in place.
- The chain row of the Return Pass makes an **upper horizontal bar** and a **lower horizontal bar.**
- There are two different spaces within a completed row. The space **between the front and the back vertical** part of the same stitch is joined at the top. It is wider at the bottom and narrower at the top.
- The space **between two stitches** is larger and looks like a small rectangle.
- The first Return Pass chain appears as Vees on the front of the fabric. The back bumps dominate the back of the row. This looks similar to the starting chain.

Each of these areas is an opportunity for hook placement to create different stitches.

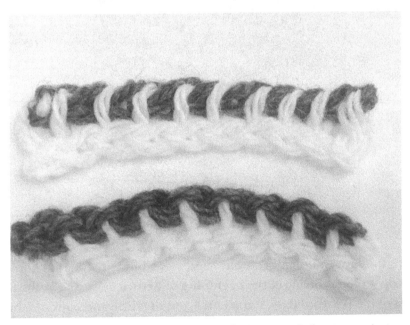

From top: Front and back structure of a foundation row is best seen in two colours.

Forward Pass and Return Pass

One row of Tunisian crochet is made in two stages.

- The **Forward Pass** places stitches onto the hook.

- The **Return Pass** removes these stitches from the hook as you chain through each one.

- The top of the Forward Pass stitch is caught by the back bump of the Return Pass. This locks the Forward Pass stitch into place.

- To see the stitch structure clearly, attach a different colour yarn before starting the Return Pass.

The **direction** of the Return Pass varies according to the project.

With a regular afghan hook, working flat, the Return Pass is made in the **opposite** direction to the Forward Pass, and the work is *not* turned.

In circular projects or working in the round using a double-ended hook, the Return Pass "**chases**" the Forward Pass stitches in the same direction. Each end of the hook has its own function and the work *is* turned.

TSS with the same number of stitches and rows, but two different hook sizes. From top: Colour change at the beginning of Return Pass, and at the beginning of the Forward Pass. From left: Front of fabric and back of fabric.

Purl and Reverse

In Tunisian crochet, the main confusion in stitch names is with the **Reverse** and **Purl** stitches, which are considered interchangeable by some. When you work these stitches in two colours changed at the beginning of the Forward Pass, you see the difference in structure. The Reverse stitch is used in shadow or Illusion Tunisian crochet. The Purl stitch is used in the Honeycomb stitch combination and to make ribbing in the delinked technique.

From top: Reverse stitch and Purl stitch. From left: Front of work and back of work.

Making Test Samples

Most of the test samples in this workbook are done in Tunisian Simple Stitch (TSS) as this is the fastest way to discover whether a hook and yarn are a good fit for each other. Consider this the "speed-dating" process before you make a huge time and/or financial commitment to begin a new project.

I often use a regular crochet hook and 10 to 12 stitches for a test sample. All of my test samples and photos are worked right-handed. I have not used "right" and "left" in the directions. I prefer to say "at the beginning of the Forward Pass" (one stitch on the hook) and "at the beginning of the Return Pass" (all the stitches are on the hook). When working with several colours of yarn, I call my working yarn the *travelling* yarn.

Explore and Discover

- Allow yourself to relax and have fun when you learn a new technique.

- Find adventure in playing with yarn.

- The TSS extended stitch is a good choice for a scarf because it makes a looser fabric. Use team colours.

- Use a larger hook and a lighter coloured yarn; this loosens up the stitches so you can see the structure clearly.

- Use two contrasting colours and change yarn at the beginning of a Return Pass to observe the stitch structure.

- Make test samples to determine the best match of hook and yarn, like "speed-dating".

- A regular crochet hook can hold about 12 stitches for a small test sample.

Use a regular crochet hook to make test samples.

- Sample a circular project into small napkin rings or bracelets.

- Sample a new stitch or technique into a dishcloth or baby bib using cotton yarn.

- Stitch width does not always equal stitch height.

- Use coloured yarn or stitch markers to identify the various positions on your work: front/back, top or north edge, bottom or south edge, and the sides or east and west edges.

- If you follow a pattern exactly and it does not work as it should, there may be an error in the pattern. Check for *errata* on the company web site.

- In Tunisian crochet, what you do in the current row will change the appearance of the completed row below.

- Repetition creates patterns.

- Learn to read your stitches and map your work. Consider the pattern as a GPS for your project. The more often you go to the same place, the more likely you will find a faster route or a nice detour without affecting the outcome.

- Know yourself, what works for you, gives you fun, excitement, and what bores you.

Techniques You Will Explore in This Workbook

- Begin and end a row or a piece of fabric
- Working into the chain
- Where and how to increase and decrease
- Joining and linking
- Making a Mobius
- How to use yarn overs on the next row
- Textures and shapes that mimic those in knitting
- Combining stitches for some unexpected results
- Interpreting knitting and crochet into Tunisian crochet
- Delinking or removing the Return Pass yarn
- Wobbel or working into rows below the usual row

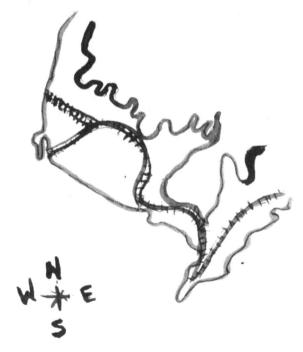

Think of your work as a map. Your yarn travels west or east in Forward and Return Passes. Your fabric progresses from south to north.

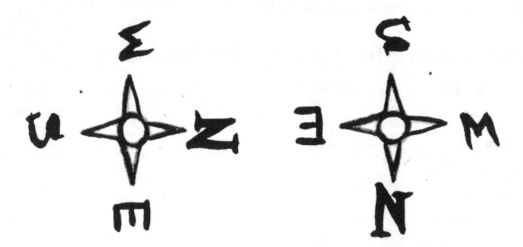

South is the starting chain and foundation row of the fabric or the section.

When you see the compass turned on its side or upside down beside a photo, it shows the actual direction of the work. This indicates that the photo has been turned sideways or upside down.

BEGIN and END

The hardest part of learning to crochet is making the first row. The foundation or starting row is usually worked into a basic chain. When you make a chain, the slip knot is the south end and you are working north in a column of single chain stitches. To work the first row into the chain, turn the chain 90 degrees on its side. Columns are south/north and rows are east/west.

You begin by picking up one of the following parts of the chain stitch:

- the upper horizontal loop only;
- the back bump only;
- both of the above together.

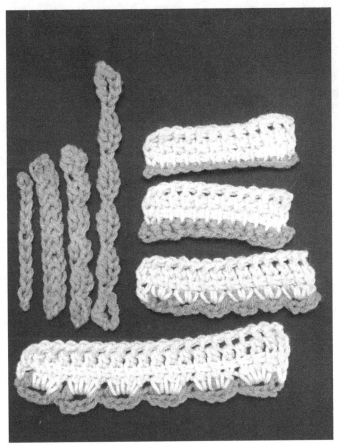

From left: Chain, 2-stitch TSS, double and treble crochet columns.
Columns are turned sideways to work the first row.

Column Foundations

Column foundations are more flexible than a column of chain stitches as a base for the foundation row. Sometimes called a "chainless" foundation, this is a narrow column of stitches made to the required length. To work the first row into this column, turn the column on its side and pick up the stitches along one long edge. The column forms the south edge of the work.

- Use a column of two Tunisian crochet stitches for a starting column with some elasticity. This is the same as if you are working the first and last stitches only of a row. This column foundation can be repeated at the top edge of the work by linking it to close the final row.

- For some textured yarns, such as bouclé and mohair, regular chain stitches may be difficult to locate and work into. Use a column of two double crochet or two treble crochet stitches and work the first row into the open spaces, placing two or more stitches into each space. You will need to use an Extended stitch or a Tunisian Double Stitch when you work into an open space or place two new stiches into the same location.

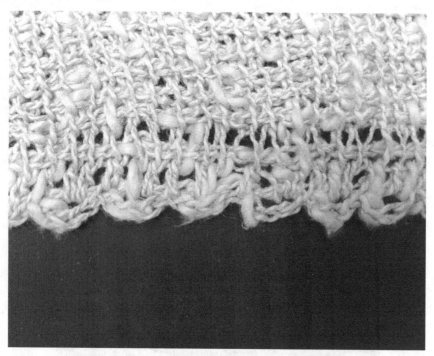

Hand towel lower edge starts with a 2-stitch double crochet column.

Side Edge Chain

Side Edge and Bottom Edge Continuous Chain

In order to make a neat edge on the side of the work where the Forward Pass ends, you can prepare by chaining enough stitches for each row of TSS in the project, place a marker, and then continue with the chain for the foundation row. Link the first stitch of the Return Pass to this side chain, one row at a time, through the back bump on the next available stitch.

Continuous chain for side edge and bottom.

Provisional Chain

A provisional chain is a temporary row of chain stitches which will be removed. It allows you to pick up stitches later, going in the opposite direction (e.g., to add a cuff or lengthen a hem).

- For a provisional starting chain, use a smooth, non-stick yarn.

- Make a provisional chain in a contrasting colour with more stitches than you will need for the work (e.g., 30 stitches for a 21-stitch piece).

- Beginning in about the third back bump, with the main colour, pick up the loops *in the back bumps*. Work the Return Pass in same main colour. **Only** by working into the back bump will this provisional chain release later.

- The last stitch of the Forward Pass needs to be locked into place in the second row. Work a TSS Relaxed stitch into the top horizontal bar of the first return chain and the last vertical stitch of the first row.

- Secure the yarn end of the first main colour stitch of the Forward Pass.

- Remove the contrast chain later when you edge or join this row in the opposite direction. The chain comes undone from the *last* stitch you made in the chain.

- If you are making a very wide piece, begin working the first/foundation row at the *tail* end of the provisional chain so that you can increase the chain at any time at the working end for a different stitch count.

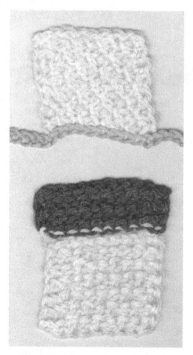

Black piece is added before provisional chain is removed.

Last Row of the Work

To finish the last row of the work, continue the final row in the stitch pattern but instead of keeping the loops on the hook, pull the second loop loosely through the first one (**slip stitch**) and repeat to the end.

- If you want to end the final row and edge the piece all at once with a single crochet stitch, use a *smaller hook*, as you are switching from Tunisian to regular crochet. This edge is more elastic than a slip stitch edge.
- If you plan to join a new section to this piece, you can leave the last row open and join the next row to these stitches in a south/north direction, or link rows in an east/west direction.

Edge Stitches

A common concern for many Tunisian crocheters is that one side edge of the work appears looser and longer than the opposite side edge. There are a few ways to manage the loose stitch at the **beginning of the Forward Pass**.

- Pull on the single stitch as it is made to tighten it, and again after the second and third stitches have been worked, removing the slack.
- Tighten and remove the first stitch from the hook and pin it to a row below until you return to it.
- Consider using a purl stitch for the second stitch of the selvedge.

The **beginning of the Return Pass** is often tighter than the Forward Pass edge.

- Work the last stitch of the Forward Pass as a stand-alone stitch and not as a pattern stitch.
- Elongate the last stitch slightly as you work it.
- As you work the first stitch of the Return Pass, use a marker to identify the two parts of the edge stitch to pick up at the end of the next Forward Pass. This will create a chain edge.
- Use a smaller crochet hook or cable needle to pick up the two parts of the stitch, then enlarge it or slide these threads onto the regular hook.

If your work will be finished with an edging, or joined to another piece, the discrepancy in side edges will not be as obvious.

Colour Changes

The location of the colour change affects the overall appearance of the fabric.

The Stitches

- At the end of the **Return Pass**, with two stitches remaining on the hook, wrap your new colour around the hook and pull it through both stitches; the resulting stitch is the first stitch of the next **Forward Pass** row.

Black yarn over and out. White yarn under and in. White will be the first stitch of the next row.

- At the end of the **Forward Pass**, wrap the new yarn over the hook and pull it through the last stitch of the Forward Pass to begin the Return Pass, then wrap and pull through two stitches as usual. The vertical stitches will be one colour; the horizontal chain will be a second colour. This is a good way to observe the mechanics of the stitch construction.

Pull new colour through first stitch to begin Return Pass.

To change the colour of the working yarn midway, the new colour is added when the final loop of the current working stitch is made.

Colour blocks are good way to practice colour changes.

The Yarn

- **Repetition** results in a pattern. Use an "over and out, under and in" repeat when changing yarns at either end or in the middle of a row.
- Over, in the same direction as yarn is travelling (east or west).
- Under, from away, from the opposite direction.
- To change colours at either end of the work: *Working colour, over and out; new colour, under and in.* This will cross them over in the same way.

If the working direction is going west, move the old colour to the west, over and out, and move the new colour to the east under the old colour and in to be used.

If the working direction is going east, move old colour to the east, over and out, and move the new colour to the west under the old colour and in to be used.

Keep the Fabric from Rolling Up

Tunisian crochet worked in all TSS or TRS has a tendency to roll up because you are always working on the same side of the fabric. There are some ways to keep the fabric flat.

Hook

- Use a hook 2 to 3mm greater than the recommendation on the ball band for the yarn.

Chain

- Use a column foundation for a more flexible first row.

In the first row

- Change the position of the **yarn** from the front to the back of the work between each stitch or a group of stitches. Use alternating TSS and TPS stitches or the half linen stitch.
- Change the placement of the **hook**. Use stitches that alternate between the front and the back like the TSS and TRS.
- **Add** one chain stitch above each completed stitch in this row (Tunisian extended stitch).

Yarn

- Block the work according to the fibre content.
- Add a backing worked from side edge to side edge as a lining across the reverse side of the fabric to keep the side edges straight.

Explore and Discover

- If you work with the yarn held double or with several yarns held together: check the back of the row occasionally to make sure you have not lost one of the loops along the way.
- It is easiest to count your stitches when all of them are on the hook.
- Leave at least a 6-inch end of yarn to weave in when you change colours or begin and end your yarn.
- Make the starting slip knot so that the short end of the yarn tightens the loop.
- If the starting chain is too tight, use a larger regular crochet hook to make the chain, and then switch to the smaller afghan hook.
- Use markers every 20 stitches when making a very long starting chain.

- For greater stretch, chain two for each stitch between the selvedges and pick up only every second stitch on the first row, plus the first and last stitch.

- The easiest part of the chain to pick up for the first row is the upper horizontal loop.

- If you pick up in the back bar on the starting row, you get a clean lower/south edge. It will be easier to pick up these edge stitches for joining or for a finished edge to be added later without holes in the edge.

- It is easier to see which stitches to pick up in the Forward Pass and which stitches to remove in the Return Pass when you change colours at the beginning of the Return Pass. This makes both parts of the stitch a different colour.

- The Haruna Cowl begins as a rectangle of TSS in two colours, changed at the beginning of the Return Pass. Join the last row to the first row, gather the top and wear it as a hat or as a cowl.

Haruna cowl or hat.

- In order to make a frilly edge, such as the top of a flower, the final Return Pass can be used to add texture. Add three or more chains between each stitch on the Return Pass. Finish at the end of the final Return Pass. Do not bind off.

- Make a hook blanket on a regular crochet hook by linking three narrow sections. Use the hook size recommended for the yarn. The fabric will roll on its own.

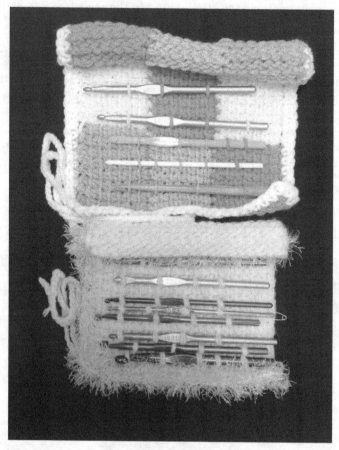

Hook blankets take advantage of the natural roll of the fabric.

The CHAIN

Making a chain is the stitch action used to begin most crocheted items. In Tunisian crochet it is also used in the Return Pass.

Return Pass

The Return Pass is a chain that **secures** the live stitches of the Forward Pass one at a time, or in groups, and holds the fabric together. It is the **back bump** part of this chain stitch that holds each Forward Pass stitch in place.

Make a Row Wider

- **Add** a chain before the next Forward Pass. With one stitch remaining on the hook, continue to chain with the Return Pass yarn to widen the edge of the work.
- **Attach** a chain before the Return Pass. With a small section of the same yarn, make a chain for the number of stitches you want to add and hold it beside the edge. As you work the Forward Pass, continue past the last stitch and work onto the chain.

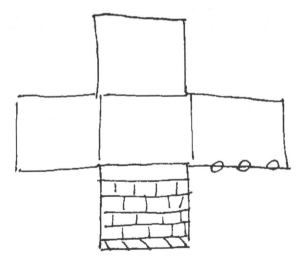

Practice attaching and adding chains to make the sides of a small box.

Buttonholes

- To create an opening, bind off one or more stitches in the Forward Pass. On the Return Pass, chain this same number of stitches above the opening, one for each stitch bound off.

- On the next Forward Pass, work the stitches directly into the chain, either the top horizontal loop, or the back bump.

- Exaggerated holes can become part of the overall pattern, as in the Dining Car Window stitch.

Relaxed Stitches

A Relaxed stitch is made on the Forward Pass by picking up a regular stitch *plus* a designated thread of the Return Pass chain. Work the Return Pass loosely.

- **Relaxed TSS:** insert the hook under the vertical bar as for a simple stitch, and then under the top horizontal bar between this and the next stitch before pulling up the new loop. This helps the fabric spread out a bit and lay flatter. TuniCrochetWeaver calls this a BirdTail Stitch.

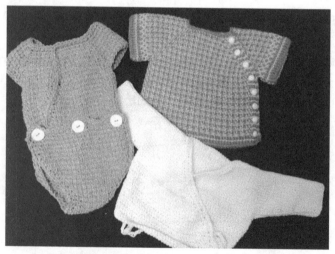

**Relaxed simple stitches are softer for baby items. Many baby clothes
start at the neck edge and are worked top-down.**

- **Relaxed TKS:** insert the hook into the next stitch as a knit stitch, and then into the bottom horizontal portion of the chain from the previous Return Pass before pulling up the new loop.

- **Relaxed Front Diagonal:** insert the hook under the front diagonal thread of a Yarn-Over and then under the top horizontal bar of the chain stitch just above it.

Mesh

Double Up in the Forward Pass and add a chain between each stitch in the Return Pass for a *mesh texture*.

- Begin with 2 chains per stitch for the base, plus one edge stitch at each side. Pick up every second stitch between the edge stitches.

- Add a chain to each stitch in the Forward Pass (Extended stitches).

- Add a chain between each stitch on the Return Pass.

- Maintain selvedges.

- When you work with thin yarn and a larger hook, this creates an open lacy texture.

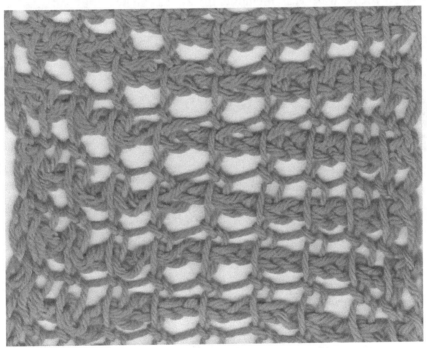

Mesh is one option for mohair, bouclé, and other textured yarns.

Explore and Discover

- Learn to recognize the direction of the work, front and back, up and down, right and left, by the direction of the Return Pass/chain row.

- Tight chains are useful for cords. Pull each stitch really close to the last one.

- Make a stretchy cord by working a chain to the required length, then slip stitching across the chain back to the starting point.

- Measure a crochet chain for the desired length of a sideways scarf or a cowl circumference by draping it around your own neck.

- The starting chain for a Mobius should reach the sternum for one wrap; double that for two wraps as the twist will affect the final circumference.

- Some yarns are difficult to use in a Forward Pass. Eyelash, popcorn, and other art yarns work well in a Return Pass that is the chain portion of the row.

- Some stitch combinations feature the chain stitches of the Return Pass. This is more obvious if the fabric is worked in two colours with a double-ended hook.

- The Reverse stitch pushes the back of the chain of the previous row to a position of prominence. This feature is used in illusion Tunisian crochet based on *Illusion Knitting (woollythoughts.com)*. Another term for Illusion Knitting is shadow knitting.

- In a 29-stitch test sample of the Dining Car Window stitch pattern, only 8 stitches remain on the hook at the end of the Forward Pass, including the 2 edge stitches. The 3 stitches for each space that were bound off on the Forward Pass must be replaced with chain stitches on the Return Pass.

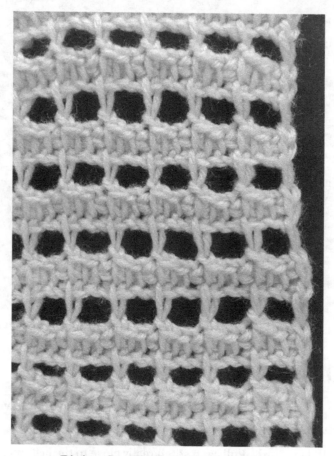

Dining Car Window stitch pattern.

INCREASES and DECREASES

Increases and decreases are used to change the shape of the fabric; to make it wider or narrower.

Selvedges

If the fabric you are making will not be joined or have an edging attached, consider keeping a *selvedge* at both edges of the fabric. This term comes from weaving and knitting, where it is used to keep the side edges of the fabric strong. The width of the selvedge will be based on the width of the fabric and can be two or three stitches wide. The pattern is worked in between the selvedges.

Begin your increase or decrease inside the selvedge at stitches 2 & 3 or even at stitches 3 & 4 for an angle. Increases and decreases placed at the *centre* of the rows are used to create shapes like leaves, with smooth outer edges. Increases and decreases *at* or *on* the edge are used when making circles.

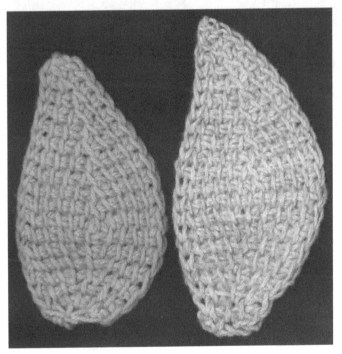

Rows with increases, then decreases, next to the centre stitch.

If you increase a stitch at one end of the row and decrease a stitch at the opposite end of the row, your fabric will slant in the direction of the increased stitch. The stitch count will be the same in every row.

Increases

Each choice will give a different appearance. Some increases will make holes.

- Work one stitch into the space between two stitches.
- Work one stitch into the upper horizontal part of the return chain, between two stitches.
- Work one stitch into the back vertical (by hooking it from the front) and another into the front vertical of the same stitch.
- Work into the second stitch away from you, work into the skipped stitch, and then work again into the second stitch (crossed increase).
- Yarn over between two stitches.

Accidental Increases: Working into the spaces between all the stitches plus the first and last stitch will increase your row stitch count by one stitch. You need to alternate where you put the second stitch on each row. Maintain the stitch count in each row.

Another common accidental increase is making an unintended yarn over between two stitches.

Decreases

Each choice will give a different appearance.

- Work two together on a Forward Pass for a one-stitch decrease.
- Work two together on a Return Pass then pick them up as one on the next Forward Pass.
- Work two taller stitches individually, and then pull the second one of this pair through the first one (bind off effect). In TSS this adds height to the stitch. It works best if using an Extended stitch or taller stitch such as a TDS or treble.
- Skip a stitch.
- Decreases near the outer edges of every row, or at every second or third row will vary the angle and produce different appearances.
- The height of a stitch will determine the angle of the decrease.
- For a double or two-stitch decrease at the same location, work 3 together on a return or Forward Pass.
- Decreasing one stitch at each side of a centre stitch forms a mitre decrease.

Accidental Decreases: Occasionally on the Forward Pass one stitch may have slipped into the previous one. The most common accidental decrease is at the beginning of the Return Pass, when two stitches are worked together at the beginning of the pass, instead of the first Return Pass stitch being worked on its own.

Explore and Discover

- Experiment with making different triangle shapes. Use paper patterns to determine when and where to make the increase or decrease.

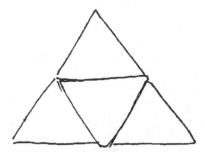

Explore paper shapes.

- A decreasing right-angle triangle is worked with decreases on the beginning edge of every row in the Return Pass.

- An increasing right-angle triangle is worked by increasing one stitch at the end of the Forward Pass in each row and linking this to the beginning chain.

- Short rows are used to make parts of the fabric wider in some places and narrower in other places. In a short row hat each section has four rows of different lengths. This makes the top of the hat narrow and the brim edge wider.

- A circle is the top of a pillbox style hat.

Hats worked sideways or top down.

- A fir tree ornament has decreases every third row to form the shape. Add yarn snow on one side and button decorations on the other side.

Decrease every third row.

- If all your test samples are made to the same dimensions, they can be stitched together later into a project.

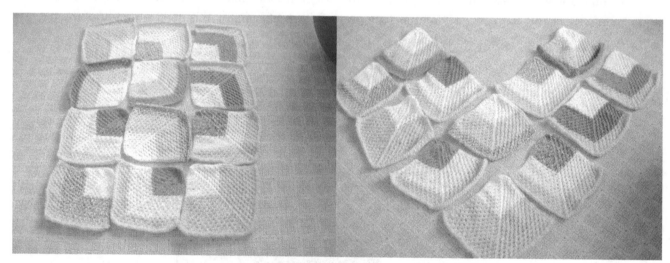

Blanket or shawl?

JOINING and LINKING

Many crocheted pieces are stitched together with a blunt needle and yarn or joined to each other with a single crochet seam. I wanted to borrow some techniques from sewing and knitting to give me more options for Tunisian joining and edging.

Joining Two Edges

To join cowls and headbands I explored ways to make the final Forward Pass and join it to the first row at the same time. Place the first row just above the final row. Both pieces are face up.

Last row meets first row for a bind off.

- Slip stitch the last row closed on the Forward Pass treating both rows as one. Hold the yarn under the two sections, below the stitches. Pick up a last row stitch plus the matching first row stitch before YOH and pull through both. This option is the one I use most often.

Slip stitch closure top left. Three full row bind-offs make thicker seams.

- Make one Forward Pass through the two stitches of both rows and one Return Pass. The appearance of the row changes if you hold the working yarn at the back of the row, in front of the row, or under the row between the two sections. Make a test sample to get the desired effect.

- Optional: Add a decorative edging such as a picot edge or frill to emphasize the seam.

- Use a row of TSS to join two side seams on knitting. Make one Forward Pass, one Return Pass, then slip stitch the row closed.

Tunisian bind off for knitted seams.

- Single crochet the rows together on the Forward Pass, using a smaller hook since you are switching from Tunisian to regular crochet.

Use an outside seam to match stripes.

Linking

Link two vertical pieces by adding another section between them.

- Start a foundation chain between two pieces by beginning in the bottom row edge stitch (left piece A if right-handed).

- When you get to the other edge (right piece B if right-handed), slip the last single stitch off the hook, and insert the hook into the corner bottom stitch of piece B then replace the chain stitch back on the hook, and pull it through B, treating these as one stitch from now on.

- Work the Forward Pass as usual, including the last stitch. Now slip the hook into the edge stitch of row 2 on piece A, and treat this and the last stitch picked up as one, YOH and pull through both of these stitches together. If you insert the hook front to back, you get a different appearance than if you insert the hook back to front. Experiment with both for the look you want to achieve.

- When you have one stitch remaining on the hook at the end of the Return Pass, slip it off briefly, insert hook from right to left (if right-handed) through the edge stitch and place the single stitch back on the hook. Pull the single stitch through the edge stitch of piece B (no Yarn Over Hook needed).

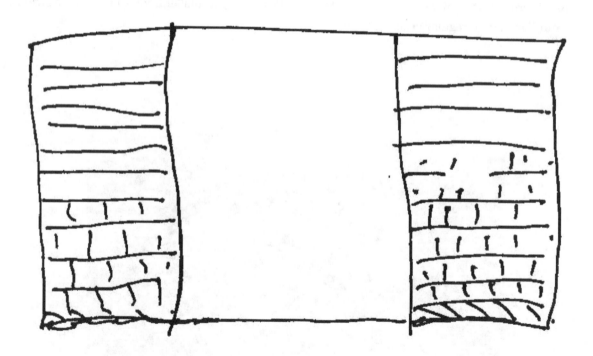

Add a section between two pieces.

- I used this method to add a gusset between the back and the front of a sweater at the side seams. I also used it in the sleeves, decreasing the width of the insert as I got near the cuff end.

Gusset in TSS between two sections of a sweater.

Linking or joining to the top of an **unfinished row** will finish the row, with no need to slip stitch it closed.

- At the end of a Return Pass, one stitch remains on the hook.

- Turn fabric 90 degrees, so the side edge and single stitch are now south.

- Chain the number of stitches for a new section (e.g., 5).

- Pick up the loops on a Forward Pass, then link the final stitch to the previous section by inserting the hook into what was the vertical second stitch of the final row. This stitch now appears to be horizontal.

- Treat the last stitch of the Forward Pass and the linking stitch as one (slip stitch).

- In some projects I change the hook size to compensate for the difference between stitch height and width.

Link to the top row.

Explore and Discover

- Use a regular crochet hook to make a linked scarf. Chain 6 stitches. Increase one stitch at the beginning of each Forward Pass (7 stitches), decrease one stitch at the beginning of each Return Pass (6 stitches), working on a 7/6 count. Make to desired length. Add a new section by linking a second chain-6 section to the first piece at lower edge. Link each row at the end of the Forward Pass to the first scarf section, row by row.

Slanted columns linked for a scarf.

MOBIUS

Are you ready to question your understanding of reality? I saw this on a poster at *Revolutions in Science,* an exhibit in Waterloo, Ontario along with a picture of a Mobius. In 2010, I came across the Mobius sculpture in a small town in the Netherlands.

Mobius sculpture in Zeeland, the Netherlands. Eb en Vloed by Piet Slegers.

Casting on stitches for a knitted Mobius is a technique described by Cat Bordhi (catbordhi.com). When I met Cat in 2010 she encouraged me to find a Mobius cast-on option for Tunisian crochet. My technique first appeared as the *Mephitis Cast-On* pattern on Ravelry in 2010. I have used it to make a variety of the Mobius items from Cat's knitting pattern books.

Felted Mobius Basket in TSS. Knitting pattern from A Second Treasury of Magical Knitting by Cat Bordhi.

A Tunisian Mobius can be worked from a centre "spine" outward in a continuous round with two colours and a double-ended hook.

Double wrap Mobius shawl.

Basic Tunisian Mobius Method

Use a **double-ended crochet hook**. The length of the hook does not matter. I use a hook size 3mm larger than recommended on the yarn wrapper. For sock yarn use at least a 6.5mm hook, for worsted weight use at least an 8mm hook and for chunky yarn use at least an 11.5mm hook. I have used the Denise cabled hooks and the double-ended birch hooks from River John Needle Company in Nova Scotia.

Use **two colours of yarn**: Colour A for the Forward Pass, Colour B for the Return Pass. The yarn can be different weights. A novelty yarn works well for the Return Pass. I recommend that you do NOT use the same yarn or the same colour for both yarns until you are familiar with the technique.

Starting Options for the Centre Spine

My preferred length for the starting chain is measured around my neck to the sternum. For a twice-wrapped Mobius, double this length and it becomes a hood plus cowl.

A. Loosely chain a row with Colour A. You will be working into both the upper and lower horizontal bars of this chain for the foundation row. Use a larger hook if necessary.

B: A column foundation works well to maintain the elasticity of the spine.

2-stitch Tunisian column.

The Foundation Row

Begin the first row as you would in working a regular Tunisian foundation row, using a TSS or extended stitch. In the column option, you will insert the hook into the edge stitches, going down one side of the column.

The first row is worked into the back of the spine edge.

When you run out of room on the hook, you can begin the Return Pass. Turn the hook so the back of the work (front of the spine) now faces you, attach Colour B and start removing loops in the Return Pass.

When you begin the Return Pass, the front of the spine faces you.

Always leave a few loops of Colour A on the hook. This may prevent you from going in the wrong direction when you pause in your work and pick it up later.

Three plus one is a good number to leave on before turning.

Turn the work to the front to pick up more stitches with Colour A for the Forward Pass, turn again to the back to continue the Return Pass with Colour B. Both yarns are going in the same direction; Colour B is "chasing" Colour A.

Make the Turn

When you get to the last stitch on the Forward Pass (at the slip knot end of the starting chain), stop. You have one edge in Colour A (the starting chain) and one edge in Colour B (the Return Pass).

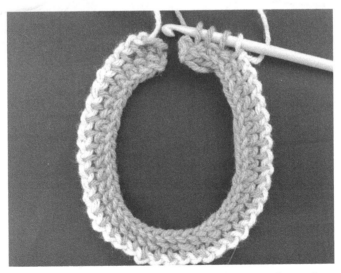

Lay your work on a flat surface to line up the ends.

First, line up the two ends to create a circle, making sure the row is flat. Now turn the free end (not on the hook) over towards you so that the unworked part of the foundation row is up.

One way to think of it is like this. Your fingers are the starting chain, and your thumbs indicate the location of the foundation row.

When you place your hands **palms up** with both **thumbs up**, and the row is flat, you could continue to work into the top of the foundation row. The result would be a **cowl**.

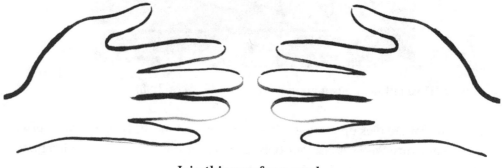

Join this way for a cowl.

To make a half twist for the Mobius, turn one hand **palm down and thumb down**, leaving the other **palm and thumb up**. The starting chain will now have one fold in it, similar to placing your two palms together.

Join this way for a Mobius.

Reposition the yarns to the back of the work.

Make sure your working yarns are both behind the hook and not wound through the centre. Continue working the foundation row into the opposite edge of the starting chain or column.

Mind the Gap

After making a few stitches on the second side of the starting chain or column, tighten the gap by pulling on these stitches.

Tighten the slack between the two ends.

Confirm the Turn

Once you have worked all of the foundation row stitches, you will meet the first foundation stitch you made. *Make sure the Mobius twist is still there.*

Correct twist is a V-shape.

If you have made a full twist or more than one twist, you will be faced with a dilemma a few rows further on! This is fun to experiment with if you have the time. You will recognize a problem when the travelling yarns get tangled around the opening.

Too many twists.

Count the Rows

Your two yarn ends are together at the centre of the starting round. Count the rows outward from the centre spine.

One row completed.

Stitch Options

You now continue in a non-stop pattern. Use any stitch or combination of stitches. I often make small test samples as napkin rings before making a scarf version. The main design decision is whether you want both sides to look the same or to have a high contrast.

Width of Mobius

For a narrow scarf, I lay the fabric across my hand and measure the width from my wrist to my fingertip. For a wider scarf, I lay the fabric across my forearm and measure from the wrist to the inner elbow. This second width works well for a double wrap covering both the head and the neck.

Options to Bind Off

    A. Use the forward pass Colour A to bind off with a slip stitch in the stitch pattern.

    B. Use both yarns together and bind off with a slip stitch, continuing in the stitch pattern. This provides a firmer edge, much like an I-cord edge in knitting.

    C. Change to a smaller hook to bind off in single crochet, or to add a picot edge or other fancy edge.

Explore and Discover

- Alternate spellings for Mobius are *Moebius* and *Möbius*.

- To help visualize the math and geometry aspects of a Mobius, make a paper version.

- A Tunisian Mobius can also be delinked or worked in a variegated yarn in linked columns on a regular crochet hook.

Delinked Mobius

If you plan to delink the Mobius, use only the main yarn for the centre spine, the Forward Pass and the bind off stitches, as you will remove all the contrast yarn used in the Return Passes. Add a contrast colour for the outer edge.

Crossed stitches slant in the direction of the Forward Pass.

Colour Blocked Linked Columns Mobius

Begin with a chain for the centre spine. Work in columns of colour or with variegated yarn and a regular crochet hook. Link each row to the spine. To add a second column, link it to the first column.

Begin a linked Mobius.

YARN OVER

A Yarn Over (YO) can be used to replace one of two stitches which are worked together. This maintains the stitch count for the row. In this type of Yarn Over you do not work it as a part of a stitch on the Forward Pass.

Yarn Over row changes the appearance of the row below.

Open Work

Yarn Over, Two Together for Open Work

After working a first row of Yarn Over/two together, you will be presented with diagonal stitches (YO from the previous row) in between the regular stitches. Identify the front diagonal and the back diagonal parts of the stitch. The back diagonal of the YO slopes up to the top. The front diagonal of the YO slopes down to the bottom.

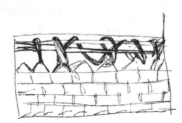

A "Yarn Over" stitch, third from left, stretches out diagonally between two vertical stitches.

Continue with Yarn Overs and use one of these options for the Two Together.

- Pick up the front vertical stitch plus the front diagonal yarn following it. YO and repeat.
- Pick up the front diagonal yarn plus the front vertical stitch following it. YO and repeat.
- Pick up the front vertical stitch plus the back diagonal yarn following it, hooking it from the front. YO and repeat.
- Pick up the back diagonal yarn plus the front vertical stitch following it. YO and repeat.
- Pick up the back and the front portions of the diagonal only and YO above the front vertical stitch without working it. Repeat.

You can work Yarn Overs in every row, or alternate a row of Yarn Overs with one or more rows of regular stitches.

Yarn Overs add interest if worked in two colours. In a solid colour the effect is lacy.

Thicker Fabric

Yarn Over in the Forward Row for thicker fabric, changing the texture:

- Start with a flexible foundation.
- Add a YO for each TSS on the Forward Pass, but not for the two selvedge stitches.
- Add the YO **after** each TSS and treat them as one stitch on the Return Pass. They appear as slopes and verticals.
  - A: If you remove the YO/TSS together in this order (slope, then vertical), you will have a straight piece of work. All of the TSS stitches are in a vertical column above each other. On the next Forward Pass pick them up in the opposite order TSS/YO (vertical, then slope).

A: Remove the YO/TSS on the Return Pass in this order: slope, then vertical.

  - B: If you remove them as TSS/YO together (vertical, then slope), the work will slant. Each vertical stitch is above a YO of the previous row. On the next Forward Pass pick them up in the opposite order YO/TSS (slope, then vertical).

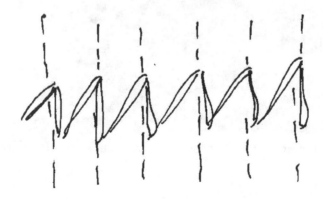

B: Remove the TSS/YO on the Return Pass in this order: vertical, then slope.

In the top section, all the vertical stitches are directly above each other. In the bottom section, each vertical stitch is directly above a sloping Yarn Over.

Tunisian Knitting Technique

This is inspired by the instructions for Tunisian knitting in the *Knitter's Handbook* (Reader's Digest, 1993) by Montse Stanley. The intent of this knitting technique is to mimic crochet. This is my Tunisian crocheted version of the knitting technique.

- Start with a foundation row in TSS. Keep one edge stitch at each end as a selvedge.

- Pattern Row 1: Slip every stitch in the row while adding a YO after each slipped stitch. On the Return Pass, treat the YO and stitch beside it as one stitch, removing them together.

- Pattern Row 2: In the Forward Pass, pick up the slipped TSS from the previous row PLUS the YO beside it as one stitch. The YO creates texture on the surface of the fabric. The TSS creates straight columns.

- Repeat Pattern Rows 1 and 2.

- This makes a thick fabric. The slipped stitches in Row 1 affect the edges of the fabric.

- To see the structure clearly, use a different colour for Row 1 and all the slipped rows.

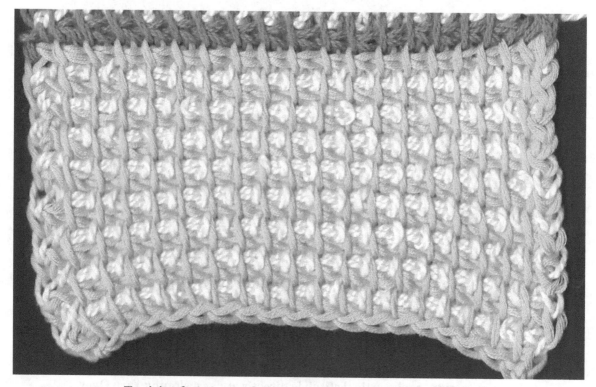

Tunisian knitting technique worked in Tunisian crochet.

Explore and Discover

- Use a knitting pattern for a bit of lace that has the "action" in one row, and a "rest" row of knit or purl for the second row. Follow the directions to create the YO and two together stitches on the Forward Pass, and the Return Pass becomes the "rest" row. Work a test sample in TSS and TKS.

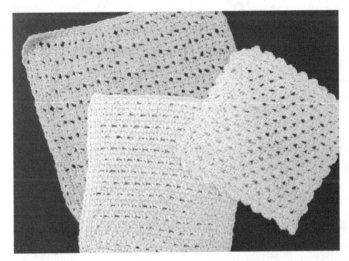

Work a series of dishcloths, one in each Yarn Over option.

- Work a cowl in any Yarn Over option, using two colours. Work every row with a Yarn Over.

- Work a cowl in any Yarn Over option, using two colours. Work every other row with a Yarn Over, using a TSS row in between.

- Add a Yarn Over after each stitch on the final forward pass to create a ruffle on an outer seam.

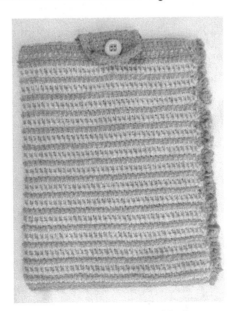

Ruffled side seam on an iPad cover.

TEXTURES and SHAPES

Knitting, crochet, and sewing use several texture techniques than can be reworked into Tunisian crochet. Pleats, hinges, folds, and gathers are more distinct if worked in a tighter fabric instead of a loose gauge.

Tunisian Rolling Pleats

Knitted rolling pleats were featured in Simply Knitting 41, May 2008. This is a Tunisian crochet method for making rolling pleats.

- Small test sample: Chain 15 stitches, work TSS 6 rows.
- Row 7: Work into the back bump above each stitch and Return Pass as usual. This causes the fabric to fold, wrong sides together, and leaves Row 6 open. You can also choose to work into the top horizontal bar but because these are offset from the stitch you will need to check to maintain the stitch count for the row.
- Work another 5 rows TSS.
- Row 13: Connect the rolling pleat. On the Forward Pass, work the back of each stitch in Row 6 together with the Forward Pass stitches in Row 13, treating Rows 6 and 13 as one row.
- Work 5 rows TSS before working into top horizontal loops again, and repeat the process.
- You can also join the pleat on a Return Pass row. Try both options to get the effect you want.
- You can alter the distance between pleats. You can place them across the full row, or alter them from side to side.

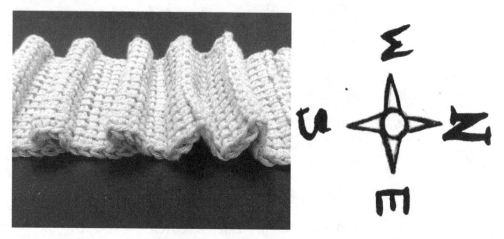

Tunisian rolling pleats and folds.

Tunisian Folds and Hinges

In knitting, a purl row can be used to fold over a stockinette hem on a skirt or top.

This technique creates hinges in Tunisian fabric that help the fabric fold into pleats.

- Fold A: On a Forward Pass, work a TRS into the *front* vertical instead of the back vertical. This brings the back sides of the fabric closer to each other with a ridge on the front.
- Fold B: From the front, work a TSS into the *back* vertical. This brings the front sides of the fabric closer to each other with a ridge on the back.

Tunisian Gathers

In sewing this technique is called shirring or ruching. In knitting it is called gathers.

- Use two hooks at least 3mm or more difference in diameter.
- Test sample: Cast on 20 stitches with the smaller hook.
- Work 4 rows.
- Change to the larger hook. Keep both edges the same, but increase each of the 18 centre stitches. Work into both the back and front vertical of each stitch, or into both the front vertical and the horizontal bar, depending on the effect you want (38 stitches).
- Work 3 more rows. On the last Return Pass row, decrease back to 20 stitches.

Change to the smaller hook and repeat.

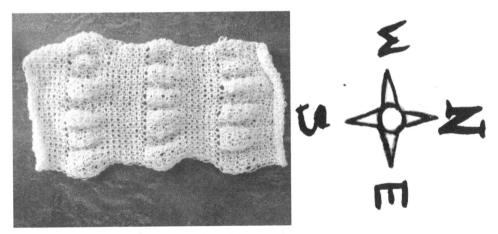

Tunisian gathers.

Tunisian Circles

Circles are made up of segments of right-angled triangles. A Tunisian circle is one way to begin a pillbox style hat. The length of the starting chain is the radius of the circle or the top of the hat.

- Make a test sample. Make one right-angle triangle with 12 stitches. The chain will be the radius with the slip knot at the centre of the circle. The beginning of the Forward Pass becomes the outer edge of the circle.

- You can make an *increasing* triangle or a *decreasing* triangle. These are mirror images of each other.

Increasing Triangle

- This triangle is worked from the narrow point toward the right-angle corner. Begin a test sample with a chain of 12 stitches.

- In the first row, work 2 stitches, then a Return Pass.

- Increase one stitch in each Forward Pass row, linking into the next available stitch in the chain through the back bump.

- In row 11 there will be 12 stitches on the hook. Make a Return Pass.

- Begin a second triangle, increasing one stitch each row by linking into the vertical stitches of the last row of the first triangle.

- Continue adding triangles until the circle lays flat.

- The right angle of the triangle is at the top end of the last row, at the beginning of the Forward Pass.

- The reverse side colour transition is smooth.

From left: Increasing triangles back and front.

Decreasing Triangle

- This triangle is worked from the right-angle corner toward the narrow point. Begin a test sample with a chain of 12 stitches.

- In the first row, work 12 stitches. To being the Return Pass, work the first two stitches together as one, decreasing **on** the edge.

- On the next Forward Pass you will pick up the two parts of this decreased stitch together as one stitch. There will be 11 stitches on the hook in Row 2.

- Continue to decrease one stitch on the edge in each row.

- In Row 11 there will be 2 stitches on the hook. Do not make a Return Pass in Row 11.

- To begin the second triangle, pick up all of the edge stitches on the decreasing slope. You will be working back toward the slip knot of the beginning chain at the centre of the circle.

- The slip knot stitch is centre of the circle. Every new triangle will have one stitch worked into this location.

- There will be 12 stitches on the hook, and each stitch will line up above the vertical stitches of the first triangle.

- Continue adding triangles until the circle lays flat.

- The right angle of the triangle is at the bottom end of the first row, at the beginning of the Forward Pass.

- The reverse side colour transition is obvious.

From top: Decreasing triangles back and front.

How many triangles does it take to make a circle?

- Circles may require from 6 to 8 triangles to lie flat depending on the number of rows per triangle and on the number of stitches in the row. The size of the hook and yarn also affects the height and width of the stitch.

- If worked correctly you will be able to follow each TSS column around the circle from segment to segment.

- When you make the first triangle, fold it to see if the two sides next to the right angle are equal. The third side will be longer. Working into the longest side of the triangle creates the swirl in the circle.

Surface Design

- The surface of a Tunisian Simple Stitch fabric can be used as a base for embroidery or other surface embellishments.

Patchwork Stars designed by Marion Graham. Afghan Book 3, Leaflet 185 Leisure Arts, 1981. Crocheted by Tove Bording.

- To add texture to a flat fabric, work one or more regular crochet stitches into each front vertical loop on the surface.

Three single crochet stitches worked into each TSS loop.

Ribbing

Tunisian crochet is not a stretchy fabric. Stitches such as the TKS and TFS provide some stretch in a south/north direction. The most stretch is working through the back bump only.

In regular crochet, working through the back loop only (BLO) adds stretch in a south/north direction. In knitting, columns of knit/purl stitches create ribbing with an east/west stretch, but this is not the case in Tunisian crochet.

Here are two versions of Tunisian ribbing. In both versions the back of the work appears to dominate the fabric.

Ribbing on an afghan hook: The work is **turned** after each rib section.

- Use TSS, TSS relaxed, TSS extended, or TDS for the stitch. Try a test sample on about 20 stitches.
- Work one Forward Pass and Return Pass.

- Slip stitch the top of this row closed: Chain one, mark this stitch, pick up the second vertical loop, yarn over and pull through both stitches on the hook. Do NOT single crochet. At the last stitch chain one and turn. The extra chain stitches are there to let the edges, as well as the rest of the stitches in the row, stretch.

- Make a Forward Pass by inserting the hook into what is now the **back** loop only (BLO) across the row. Begin by working into the second stitch from the edge. Maintain the stitch count. The last stitch will be made into the marked stitch. Make a Return Pass, bind off, etc. This switches the pattern from the back of the fabric to the front of the fabric on each section. The back of the row is the dominant appearance of the rib section.

- Using the BLO makes the fabric stretchy in a south/north direction.

**From bottom: TSS ribbing has more texture than TSS Relaxed ribbing.
Linked rows of back bump stitches across the north edge.**

Ribbing with a double-ended hook: The work is **turned** after each Forward Pass.

- Work in two colours. Each colour will dominate one side of the fabric. Note that the dominant colour shows on the side of the Return Pass.

- Test sample: Chain 20 and work a Forward Pass with Colour A. Turn the hook. Slide the work to the opposite end of the hook and attach Colour B. Make a Return Pass from this end.

- With Colour B, pick up in the top horizontal loop only across the row. Do not work into the edge stitch. Maintain a stitch count of 20. Turn the hook. Make the Return Pass with Colour A from the opposite end.

- The fabric will be stretchy in a south/north direction.

- For a wrist warmer, wrap the stretch around the hand and join the seam. Leave an opening for the thumb.

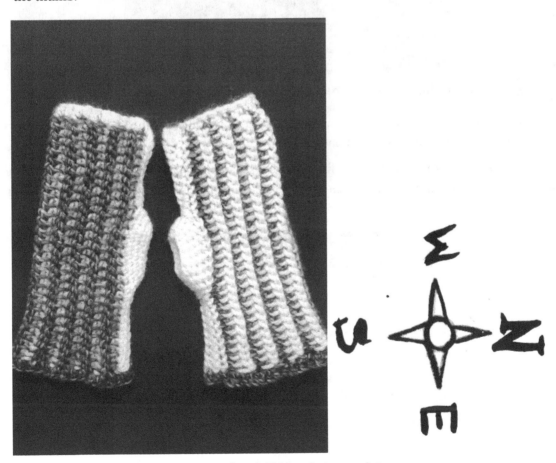

Turn a rectangle of ribbing into a wrist warmer.

Explore and Discover

- For more circle options, search for words such as Tunisian "pinwheels", "circle dishcloths", "wedges", or "short rows".

Begin a hat, a basket, a bag, or a flower with a circle as the base.

- Make a headband on a regular crochet hook. Begin with 12 stitches for the width and work the rows in TKS until the fabric fits. TKS has a natural stretch.

- To rework a knit or crochet technique, first work a test sample in the original instructions to understand the structure, and then apply the concept to Tunisian crochet. This may mean turning the direction of the work sideways, such as in the ribbing techniques or when following graphs.

Working sideways means fewer yarn ends later.

- Turn three squares into an Oddball. Use wool that will felt. Work loosely. Join and stuff with wool. Toss it into the washer and dryer to shrink it. If you work too tightly, the shape will not change into a ball. Tunisian fabric felts very well if it is worked loosely.

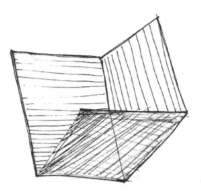

Oddball shape.

Oddballs can be used as wool dryer balls or as toys.

COMBINATIONS

Stitches worked as combinations will behave differently than a whole row or columns of the same stitch. Try any of these suggested combinations to explore the differences.

Appearance

Stitch **appearance** will change based on several things:

- an odd or an even number of stitches in the row;
- worked flat or in the round;
- using one colour for each Forward Pass, and a second colour for each return Pass;
- working a Forward Pass and a Return Pass in the same colour.

Select a stitch combination to explore in depth. Use the same stitch combination in a variety of ways: with an afghan hook; with a double-ended hook; over an even number of stitches; over an odd number of stitches; worked flat; worked in the round.

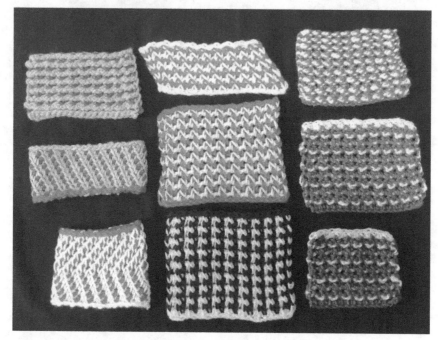

Variations on the same stitch combination: TFS/ TSS 2 together.

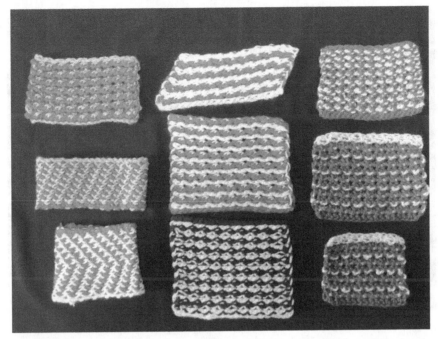

Some are the same on both sides; others have a very different appearance.

Tunisian Mock Rib

This mock rib is a combination of TSS and Twisted TSS stitches. I first discovered it as *bicolour mock-rib* in Mon Tricot Knitting Dictionary 1030 Stitches, 1972.

- Worked on a multiple of two stitches, plus selvedges.
- Use two colours. Add the second colour at the beginning of the Return Pass.
- Row 1: Colour A. *TSS, Twisted (hook up)*. Repeat.
- Row 2: Colour B. *Twisted (hook up), TSS*. Repeat.
- Repeat rows 1 and 2. The twisted sets will appear above each other in columns of colour.

From left: Mock rib stitch front and back.

- Try this while changing colour at the beginning of the Forward Pass for a different appearance.
- Work this in one colour in columns. Repeat only Row 1 in a solid colour.

Mock rib in a solid colour.

Tunisian Purl Two, Cross Two

This has become one of my favorite stitch combinations. This combination is worked flat on a multiple of 4 stitches plus selvedges. It is worked in the round on a multiple of 4 stitches plus 2.

- Cross Two: Skip 1, work the next stitch, and then go back and work the skipped stitch.

- Row 1: *Purl 2, Cross 2* and repeat.

- Row 2: Purl each of the previous crossed stitches and cross the previous purled stitches.

- Row 3 to end: Repeat Row 2.

- In 2 colours this creates an interesting front with a lattice back. In a solid colour this adds texture to the fabric.

- Options: Shift over by 1, 2, or 3 stitches in the next round for a different appearance. Begin with a multiple of 4 plus the desired shift (1, 2, or 3).

- When you cross the two stitches, the skipped purl may be difficult to relocate on the next row.

From top: Purl two Cross two, front and back.

Purl two Cross two cowl.

Tunisian Half Linen Stitch

This stitch is based on the half linen stitch in knitting.

- Try TSS, TKS, or TRS for the working stitch.
- Row 1: Forward Pass *work 1, yarn forward, slip 1, yarn to back*, repeat. Return Pass as usual.
- Row 2: Forward Pass *yarn forward, slip 1, yarn to back, work 1* repeat. Return Pass as usual.
- This makes a stiffer fabric.
- The row height is affected by the slipped stitches.
- Use variegated yarn for a different effect.

Half linen stitch in TSS.

Explore and Discover

- Much of Tunisian crochet is as nice on the back of the fabric as on the front. Make a two-sided scarf or shawl with one of the combinations.

- Make a scarf double the desired width and seam it closed on the long edge. Wear it Inside Out or Outside Out on different days.

- The mock rib stitch in two colours is a good *Inside Out Scarf* stitch combination.

- Check the bottom line: Pay attention to the row below for rows with alternating stitches such as TSS and TRS or TPS. Some stitches pull sideways and may be difficult to locate when you work the next row.

- Some stitches are best used in combinations. A solid fabric piece worked in TPS leans to one side. The same fabric worked with alternating stitches will behave differently.

- Use different yarns in combination: Try a wool yarn that will felt with a novelty yarn that will not felt and make a toy such as a ball, or an accessory such as a purse.

When you make a cowl with a double-ended hook, all of the Forward Pass stitches are on the "right" side or the outside, and the Return Pass stitches are on the "wrong" side or the inside. When you see this illustrated, it appears as a close relative of computer language, with 1 on the outside and 0 on the inside. On a train trip in 2012, a computer programmer joined the activity group. We had an interesting discussion, comparing the process of knitting, with its knits and purls, to computer coding and programming.

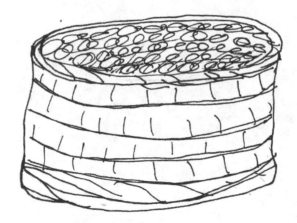

Simple stitch is 1 and chain stitch is 0 in this cowl.

INTERPRETATION

There are fewer patterns available specifically for Tunisian crochet than for knitting or regular crochet. It is possible to use patterns designed for sewing and knitting, or even an item of clothing itself, to create wearable items in Tunisian crochet. One advantage of Tunisian crochet is that you can adapt the project dimensions while your work is in progress. You can try the item on when you are down to the first stitch in the Forward Pass, or down to three stitches while working in the round.

Body Language

Learn to use your own body parts as measuring tools. Your hand is a useful measuring tool.

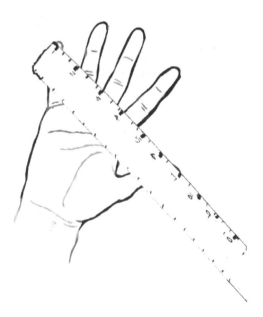

Know how to measure 4 inches, 6 inches, and 8 inches on your own hand span.

The length from the wrist to the inner elbow is the same as the person's foot length. This is also a good width for a cowl.

- Use the shoulder width for a narrow scarf.
- Measure from the top of the head to the lower neck edge or from the fingertip to the elbow, for a wider scarf.

The height of the person is the same as the fingertip to fingertip measure with arms held out straight.

Using Sewing or Knitting Patterns

You can create a piece of Tunisian fabric to a sewing pattern dimension for a **woven** fabric garment as the results are similar. Tunisian fabric is closer to woven fabric than to knit fabric because of the lack of stretch.

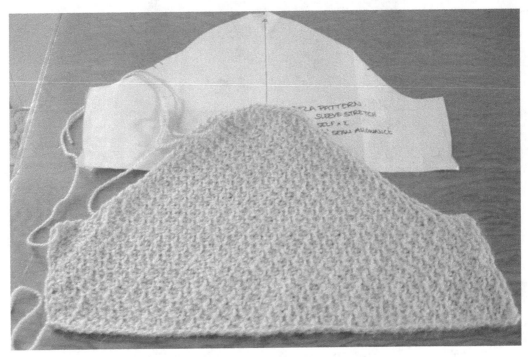

Shape a sleeve to a paper sewing pattern.

When **interpreting knitting patterns into Tunisian crochet,** use one row of Tunisian crochet (Forward Pass plus Return Pass) to represent two rows of garter stitch knitting; also called one ridge.

- A lace knitting pattern with all of the "action" in one row such as on the RS (right side) and with all WS (wrong side) rows purled, or a garter stitch which counts ridges instead of rows can be followed almost stitch for stitch, but will have a different effect using TSS or TKS.

Vortex Six Dishcloth in TSS. Knitting pattern by Rebecca Hudson on Ravelry.

TSS Fishtail Stitch II from the knitting instructions in Mon Tricot 1100 Stitches 1978.

Tunisian Illusion Crochet

Illusion knitting (*woollythoughts.com*) uses two contrasting colours and a design created by the placement of raised stitches in contrast to flat stitches. To adapt this to Tunisian Illusions, you need to focus on how the reverse stitch is formed and where the raised stitch is located.

- Work a test sample in black and white, with the illusion shape in white.
- Work in TRS to create raised stitches and in TSS to create flat stitches.
- Change the colours at the beginning of the Forward Pass.
- Move the old colour "over-and-out" and bring the new colour "under-and-in".
- Work the stitches in **this** row to change the **appearance** of those in the row below.

Origami Tzuru has detailed written instructions for *Converting Illusion Knitting into Illusion Tunisian Crochet* (Ravelry 2012).

White Tunisian Illusion Circle on a black background.
Knitting pattern by Steve Plummer on Ravelry.

Back of the fabric shows the pattern in reverse.

Explore and Discover

- Find knitting patterns with diagrams. This is a good way to work to measurements using your own stitch pattern while following the knitting instructions.

- Make a paper pattern of a well-fitting garment and use it as a pattern, or use the garment itself. This also allows two people to work on the same garment.

- If you make one test sample with the same number of stitches and rows as another test sample, they will not be the same size if they are worked in different stitches.

- Some older patterns call each Forward Pass and each Return Pass a separate row, or name the two parts as row 1A and 1B. More recent patterns will consider a row complete after having performed both a Forward Pass and Return Pass.

- Depending on the stitch used, the Forward Pass often uses from 1.5 to 3 times as much yarn as the Return Pass.

- One major difference between knitting and Tunisian crochet is the direction of the stretch in the fabric.

- Use a simple knitted slipper or baby bootie pattern and follow the directions to make a Tunisian crocheted version. Note the difference in fabric drape.

- Two rows count as one ridge in Elizabeth Zimmermann patterns (Schoolhouse Press). Many of EZ patterns can be followed exactly as written for a Tunisian version of the same garment. I have crocheted the Baby Surprise Jacket (BSJ) several times.

Elizabeth Zimmermann booties and a Baby Surprise Jacket.

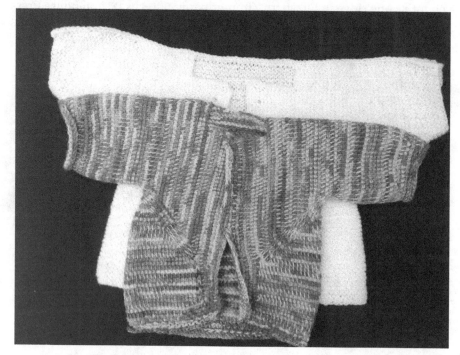

I first knit the BSJ to understand how it was constructed.

DELINK

Delink: Break the connection between (something) and something else (from the Oxford dictionary)

Working into the *back bump* on a provisional chain allows you to remove the provisional chain later. The component of the Return Pass that secures the Forward Pass stitch is the back bump of the chain. I explored and developed my Delink technique after the Return Pass **accidentally** came undone during the making of a Tunisian crochet cowl. My father named this technique a *Pull-it-Surprise*.

Unvented

Elizabeth Zimmermann used the term "unvented" to describe a technique that is not necessarily new, but waiting to be rediscovered.

This "mistake" opened a whole new set of possibilities when I explored it further. The delink technique is more successful under certain conditions.

Hook Size

Tunisian crochet requires a larger hook for the density of the fabric. If you plan to remove the Return Pass chain after completion, this changes the requirement for the hook size. Use a hook size recommended for the knitting needle on the ball band.

When Tunisian crochet is worked in the round or in a circular direction, the Return Pass is a continuous chain, which locks down the vertical stitches but is not locked down on its own. ***Under certain conditions***, this chain can be completely removed and leaves a fabric that looks remarkably like knitting.

- If the Return Pass chain becomes part of the structure of the stitch, such as in a full or knit stitch where the Forward Pass yarn wraps around the chain of the Return Pass, removing the Return Pass will be more difficult.

- Yarn Over stitches are often only held in place by the Return Pass. Delinking these stitches can make an unusual lace effect.

- Use a more flexible starting chain or a column foundation row when working a delinked cowl or Mobius.

How stitches appear when delinked compared to knitting stitches:

- Simple (TSS) and Reverse (TRS) both appear as a *knit* stitch.

- Purl (TPS) appears as a *purl* stitch.

- TSS and TPS appear as *ribbing* (in columns) or as *seed* stitch (if alternating).

- Knit (TKS) appears as *knit*, but stitches are harder to delink as the Return Pass chain is woven through the row.

- Crossed stitches appear as *slanted knit*, leaning in the direction of the Forward Pass.

Delink with a Double-ended Hook

This delinked technique is worked in the round or in a circular project with a double-ended hook.

- 30-50 stitches are a good test sample size for a small project in the round. Use a centre out knitting pattern for a circular delinked project. This will begin with 4 to 6 stitches.

- Use the hook size recommended on the ball band for the knitting needles. This is smaller than you would normally use for regular Tunisian crochet. The fabric will be stiff to work.

- Use a smooth yarn in a contrasting Colour B for the Return Pass, which acts as a provisional chain only. Using a different colour makes it easier to avoid working into the chain stitches.

- Use a double-ended Tunisian hook and crochet a piece in the round or centre-out using 2 colours. Colour A is used for the *starting* chain, all *Forward Pass* stitches and the *bind off*. Colour B is used only in the Return Pass.

- End the piece by *binding off* in Colour A.

- Pull out Colour B (it comes undone easily) and see what happens.

- When you first try this, use only those stitches which are locked down in each row, or connected to each other by stitches which will not be delinked. Extended stitches create a lace effect. Skipped or missed stitches create a run, as they would in knitting.

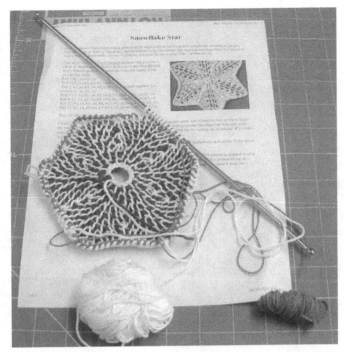

Tunisian Snowflake Star in progress. Knitting pattern by Judy Gibson on Ravelry.

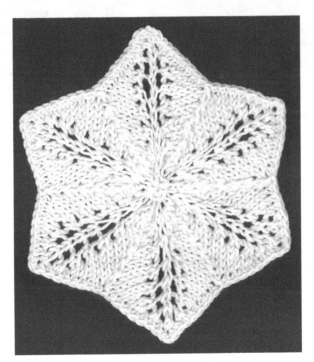

Snowflake Star delinked.

Top: Delinked crossed stitches.

Bottom: Return Pass is still in place.

Tunisian OpArt is worked from the centre out. Knitting pattern by Melissa Dominguez on Ravelry.

Delinked, the fabric lies flat.

Delink with an Afghan Hook

This delinked technique is worked flat with an afghan hook.

- The work is TURNED.

- Columns of TSS/TPS become ribbing; however, the stitch appearance is twisted.

- All rows worked in TSS become garter stitch.

- Use a smooth yarn in a contrasting Colour B for the Return Pass, which acts as a provisional chain only. Using a different colour makes it easier to avoid working into the chain stitches.

- Use the main Colour A for all Forward Pass stitches, made in an east/west direction for Row 1.

- Use Colour B for all Return Pass stitches made in a west/east direction for Row 1.

- At the end of Row 1, take the last Colour B stitch off the hook (optional: secure it with a pin).

- TURN the work. There are currently no stitches on the hook.

- With the back of Row 1 facing you, insert the empty hook under the stitch at the end of the previous Forward Pass, pull up a loop with Colour A, and continue to work another Forward Pass with Colour A.

- When all of the loops are on the hook, make a Return Pass with Colour B.

- Continue until you are ready to bind off. Bind off with Colour A.

Explore and Discover

- Work a Delink ribbing test sample in TSS and TPS columns. Try different size hooks to get a ribbing similar to knitting. The columns of knit stitches will appear twisted.

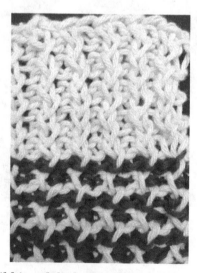

Ribbing delinks from the top down.

- Make a small test sample delinked napkin ring on about 30 stitches. Make note of how you would change the cast on, bind off and perhaps hook size to complete a full sized cowl.

- Make a delinked cowl.

Market bag. You decide in advance when and where to delink the rows.

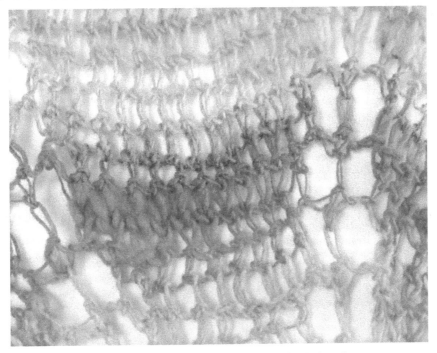

TSS extended stitches in a delinked shawl.

WOBBEL

Wobbel is the phrase I use for this technique and stands for *Work **O**ne row **B**elow the row **BEL**ow*.

Tunisian crochet is normally worked into the completed row below, changing the appearance of that row. This technique uses two stitch heights, two colours alternating in rows, and works into stitches **two** rows below. Tunisian Wobbel is inspired by the *Knit One Below* knitting technique featured by Elise Duvekot. The knitted version is quite stretchy; the Tunisian crocheted version is not. The appearance on the back of the work changes, depending on the stitch combination used.

Tunisian Wobbel

- Select your stitch combination of one short and one tall stitch.
- **Short stitch options are:**
  - TSS;
  - TKS;
  - *Slip-a-stitch*, keeping it on the hook. Note: This is different from a *slip stitch* which is pulled through the previous stitch to bind off stitches.
- **Tall stitch options are:**
  - TSS can be tall when used with slip-a-stitch;
  - TSS extended stitch;
  - TKS extended stitch;
  - Tunisian double stitch (TDS).
- Use Colour A for the foundation row.
- Change to Colour B at the beginning of the next Forward Pass. Work every even stitch as one of the *short stitch* options and work a *tall stitch* with B into the odd stitches of the foundation row.
- Next Forward Pass, change to Colour A. Work a *short stitch* into the Colour B tall stitches from the previous row, and work a *tall stitch* into Colour A stitches two rows below.
- The two colours appear in columns on the front of the fabric.

Tunisian Extended Knit Wobbel

- TKS extended and slip-a-stitch combination in two colours.

- The colour is changed at the beginning of each Forward Pass.

- The Foundation row is an odd number of stitches to balance the vertical columns. Set up the foundation row in TSS with Colour A.

- Set up Row 2 with TSS in the second colour B.

- First Wobbel row: With Colour A, work TKS extended into the same coloured stitch 2 rows below, slip all odd stitches. The stitches will be alternating colours on the hook. Maintain edge stitches as normal.

- Next Wobbel row: With Colour B, slip the even stitches and TKS extended into the same colour 2 rows below.

- The front will show vertical stripes; the back will have a wavy design.

TKS extended/slip-a-stitch combination Wobbel.

Tunisian Double Stitch Wobbel

- TDS and TSS combination in two colours.

- Colour is changed at the beginning of each Forward Pass.

- The Foundation row is an odd number of stitches to balance the vertical columns. Set up the foundation row in TSS with Colour A.

- Row 2 in Colour B: Into the even stitches work a TDS; into the odd stitches work a TSS. All the stitches on the hook are the same colour.

- Row 3 in Colour A: work a TSS into the even stitches where the TDS is in the previous row. Work a TDS into the same coloured stitch, two rows below, in every odd stitch. All the stitches on the hook are the same colour.

- The front will show vertical stripes, the back will display horizontal stripes.

TDS/TSS combination Wobbel with multiple colour transitions.

Explore and Discover

- Explore what happens when you change the colour at the beginning of the Return Pass.

- It is important to make a test sample to get the feel of the Wobbel colour changes.

- Use different tall/short stitch combinations.

- With two colours, alter the number of rows in each colour (e.g., two rows dark, one row light). Work into the stitch heights, not into the same colours below.

Front of TDS Wobbel 2 plus 1.

Back of TDS Wobbel 2 plus 1.

- Use three colours. Try five colours.

- Insert a two-row Wobble section into a regular piece of Tunisian crochet. Space the wobbles 2, 3, 4, or more stitches apart.

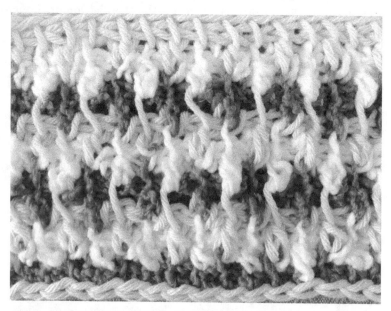

Multi-colour Wobbel in TDS/TSS combination.

Back of multi-colour Wobbel in TDS/TSS combination.

The Adventure Continues

Explore and Discover

Read the **ball band** information.

Explore **Bloop** knitting, named by Mary Lee Herrick on her website *Conditional Knitting*.

Put **buttonholes** around the edge of a shawl. Add **buttons** to create many options for wearing.

Combine regular crochet and Tunisian crochet in the same project.

Complex patterns will be lost in textured yarns such as bouclé. Use a simple stitch to feature the yarn and not the stitch.

Constraint Satisfaction: You can have fun with remnants or leftovers. You don't always need something new to make an item. Perhaps there is more creativity when you have restrictions. Look outside of the craft to get ideas such as the "quilter's challenge".

Cutting up and not coming undone: In needlework magazines from the 1800's, directions were given to create a rectangle of Tunisian crochet fabric to take to the tailor to be made up into a man's vest. Try cutting up a swatch to see what happens.

Cross-pollination: Transfer ideas and techniques from other needlework or artistic media.

Use your **cultural** experience, or ethnicity, to create one-of-a-kind projects.

Manage the **drape** of your fabric by adjusting the yarn or the hook size.

"Each one teach two" is a project of the Craft Yarn Council of America.

Tunisian **entrelac** can be worked on a regular crochet hook.

Experiment with different hook sizes in the same yarn.

Use two different size **hooks** in one project, alternating rows or sections.

Use two same size hooks if the row does not all fit onto one hook.

Start an **international** yarn collection for a special project (i.e., by country or by continent).

Intuition: When something feels wrong, listen to the nudge and investigate.

Jazzknitting with hand dyed yarns is described by Ilisha Helfman at her website followthethread.com.

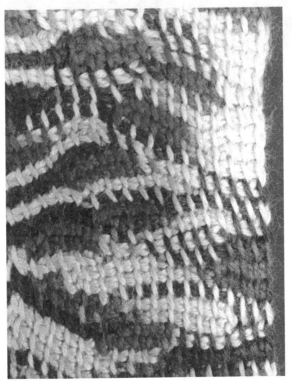

Inspired by Bloop knitting and Jazzknitting.

Job Jar: Write some interesting instructions on bits of paper and choose these at random as you are exploring. Try some of these phrases - change colour, use another stitch, change direction.

Join a knitting group for inspiration.

Knit in Public.

Knitting dictionaries provide hours of exploration and discoveries.

Let the yarn speak to you. Does it give you the results you want when you make your test sample?

Proper **lighting** is essential as you work.

Mistakes can become design features.

After a "mistake" in row three, Claro's cowl featured many more experimental stitches.
This was an amazing first Railway Knitting project on the train in November 2012.

Modify a pattern to use a new stitch or technique.

Add some **novelty** yarns to your project.

Work **outdoors** in the fresh air and sunshine.

Project versus **Process**: Some people prefer to make things; others prefer the process of making.

Ask yourself **questions** as you work. Why is this working or not working well? What could I change to improve the process?

Consider the **recipients** of your projects. What is their style, preferred colours, ease of care, and idea of usefulness?

Recycle and **Repurpose** yarns from other projects.

Scrumbling is another term for freeform crochet.

Insert a **secret code** into a special occasion project. The number of stitches or rows could represent a birthdate, a wedding date or the letters of a person's name.

When you travel, bring home **souvenir** yarn to make a project for yourself.

Make a test **sample** and learn a stitch pattern in cotton dishcloth. Is it worth the effort? Is it comfortable to do? Sample the gauge and the pattern in the actual yarn. Does it create the look you want?

Test a new idea or **technique** into a consistent size block to be joined together later into a new project.

Keep track of the **time** required to make a project or number of stitches.

Enjoy **unexpected** results when you try out a new idea.

Use what you have; use the nature of the stitch or the yarn as part of the design.

Use the colours of a **variegated** yarn to determine a change in the direction of the work, or in the type of stitch.

Use a digital kitchen scale to determine how much your test sample **weighs**, then weigh your yarn allocation to see if there will be enough yarn for the project.

Use two different **weights** of yarn in one project.

X represents crossed stitches. Skip one stitch, work the second stitch, and then work the first one.

EXtended stitches add height and change the appearance of the row.

Learn how to determine the **yarn** content with a burn test.

Mix **yarn blends** in the same project: Make a test sample, wash and dry this to see what will happen with an accidental machine wash and dry.

Yarn Landscaping: adding colour and texture to the environment. This alternate term for "yarn bombing" and "yarn graffiti" was suggested by a participant on the train in December 2011 as a more appropriate phrase to use while travelling on public transportation.

**Downtown, a song in Tunisian crochet, installed for the
Integrate Arts Festival in Victoria BC, 2014.**

Yarn is spun and plied with either an S-twist or a **Z-twist.**

Yarn is placed around a knitting needle in a **Z direction**, from the inside to the outside (south to north). Yarn is placed around a crochet hook in an S direction, from the outside to the inside (north to south).

Resources

Check out some of the following for more inspiration in Tunisian Crochet.

All Free Crochet website

The Crochet Crowd.com

Crochet Me

Freeform crochet

The **Golden Ratio**

Gutenberg pattern collection

Hyperbolic crochet

Japanese crochet symbols and videos

Knit Denise video tutorials and cabled hooks

Math and crochet

Moogly

Ravelry

River John Needle Company makes double-ended birch hooks

TuniCrochetWeaver experiments with the formation of new Tunisian crochet stitches.

CPSIA information can be obtained
at www.ICGtesting.com
Printed in the USA
LVHW05*1503230718
584649LV00020B/371/P